DAVID ADAM

Candle Prayers

Reflective services for living in the light

kevin mayhew

kevin mayhew

First published in Great Britain in 2010 by Kevin Mayhew Ltd
Buxhall, Stowmarket, Suffolk IP14 3BW
Tel: +44 (0) 1449 737978 Fax: +44 (0) 1449 737834
E-mail: info@kevinmayhewltd.com

www.kevinmayhew.com

ISBN 978 1 84867 314 4
Catalogue No. 1501248

Cover design by Rob Mortonson
Edited by Rebecca Henning
Typeset by Richard Weaver

Printed and bound in Great Britain

Contents

About the author

David Adam was the Vicar of Lindisfarne, off the Northumbrian coast, for thirteen years until he retired in March 2003. His work involved ministering to thousands of pilgrims and other visitors. He is the author of many inspiring books on spirituality and prayer, and his Celtic writings have rekindled a keen interest in our Christian heritage.

Introduction

Ever since humans discovered the use of fire and the ability to keep light burning, light has been a symbol of power and of hope. To have light was a sign of security and of triumphing over the darkness. For most people the light was in the form of a very simple oil lamp, a rush light or a candle.

It must be noticed that, in the Genesis story of creation, God is God of both darkness and light, day and night; there is no dualism which makes areas which are not God's (Genesis 1:4, 5). God is to be found in the dark as well as in the light. The lighting of a candle or a light in times of darkness should remind us of the abiding presence, power and love of God. Over the centuries candle-lighting has been used in many ways, not only as a sign of the eternal presence but at special events such as a thanksgiving or a celebration of joy; candles are lit at birthdays and at baptisms, at weddings and at funerals. We sometimes light candles as an affirmation that 'light is stronger than darkness' and sometimes as a plea that God will disperse the darkness within us or about us. We light a candle as a prayer for others or for ourselves. If this is done in a church we often leave while our 'prayer' still burns on. Candles have often been put in windows to guide people home and we still light candles in a plea for guidance.

From the earliest times fire and light were used in religious services as signs of the presence of God, and as a thanksgiving to God for the giving of a new day or for protection through the night. In the Old Testament we hear of the ceremonial attending to the lamps both morning and evening (Exodus 30:7, 8)

Every Friday evening, the beginning of the sabbath, the Jewish family gathers together to say a blessing over the lighted candles as a sign the sabbath has started. As the wife generally has more influence over the spirit of the home, she was given the privilege of lighting the Shabbat candles. If a man lives alone, then he should light the candles. The most common custom is to light two candles. However, some homes light an additional candle for each child in the family, and others light seven candles for each day of the week or for the temple's seven-branched menorah. After lighting the candles, the woman covers her eyes with her hands and recites the blessing: 'Blessed are you, Lord our God, King of the universe, who has made us holy through his commandments and commanded us to kindle the sabbath light.'

Only after the blessing is recited does the woman uncover her eyes and look at the light. By covering her eyes, the woman can focus more fully on the blessing and can postpone the enjoyment of the fruits of the blessing (seeing the light) until after the blessing is recited. Some women add a silent prayer for the family after the blessing.

On the evening of the first day of the Feast of Tabernacles the ceremony of the Illumination of the Temple took place in the Court of Women. In the centre four great golden lamps were made ready; each lamp had four golden bowls. When darkness began these four lamps are lit and, it was said, they sent such a blaze of light throughout Jerusalem that 'every courtyard was lit by their brilliance'. The obvious psalm for this occasion is Psalm 27, which begins, 'The Lord is my light and my salvation; whom shall I fear? The Lord is the stronghold of my life; of whom shall I be afraid?' It was while present at this ceremony that Jesus said, 'I am the light of the world. Whoever follows me will never walk in darkness but will have the light of life' (John 8:12).

For eight days on the festival of Hanukkah in Jewish homes, a nine-branch candle, called the menorah, is lit with prayer – one more candle each night. The ninth candle is called the shamash, which means the guardian or the servant. It is the central candle and usually stands higher or lower than the others; this candle is used to light the others. The menorah is usually placed in the window of a house or even at the entrance, for it is meant to be 'for illumination that shines out of the house upon the darkness of the world'. It is a witness to the faith that gives hope to the world and to God who is there even in the darkest times.

In the seventeenth century George Herbert told us of an old custom of asking God to bless the congregation with light from heaven as the church candles were lit.

> Another old Custome there is of saying, when light is brought in, 'God send us the light of heaven'; And the Parson likes this very well; neither is he affraid of praising, or praying to God at all times, but is rather glad of catching opportunities to do them. Light is a great Blessing, and as great as food, for which we give

> thanks: and those that thinke this superstitious, neither know superstition, nor themselves.
>
> *George Herbert,* A Priest to the Temple

It is a pity we do not have a little ceremony at each service for the lighting of candles. At Advent and Easter it is even more important to have a special lighting of the candle or candles. In the evenings we could use the Third Collect from Evensong in the *Book of Common Prayer*: Lighten our darkness, we beseech thee, O Lord; and by thy great mercy defend us from all perils and dangers of this night; for the love of thy only Son our Saviour, Jesus Christ. Amen.

While I lived on the North Yorkshire moors, I found a lovely symbolism of light from the Methodists who once lived in the area. They had a meeting place on one of the highest points of the moor at Trough House at the head of Fryup Dale. And people came from outlying farms and hamlets, from the dales of Westerdale, Danby Dale, Farndale, Glaisdale, Rosedale and Great and Little Fryup. It made Trough House look like the centre of a web that spread out into each moorland valley. Often in the late autumn they struggled up to the moorland height and met in a shuttered room. As each family entered they would light their lantern (a good symbol of receiving the light of the gospel and the light of Christ). Once the service was over they would set off in every direction. You could see the light they had received being carried with them as they travelled to each dale, to farms and homes. From that light they would see in the dark and light other lights. This light was a symbol of how they sought to live by the light of Christ. These ordinary folk were rightly known locally as 'the Lantern Saints'. I hope we may also reveal the light of Christ in our lives.

To get the best out of candle lighting it is important not to rush the occasion but to savour it. As a beginning it is necessary to fix a place and a time. To have a regular fixed place and time for our prayers is important, for without this we are in danger of soon having 'no time' and no place to pray. For many it has been beneficial to light a candle to remind them of God's presence whenever they come to pray. You might like to choose a special candle and holder for this purpose.

Candle-lighting is an act of faith. It is affirming our belief that God is here with us, that God loves us and gives himself to us. Candle-lighting does not make God come, for God is already with us.

It helps to open our hearts and minds to his coming. Candle-lighting does not make God do things that would be magic! God is already active in our lives and through candle-lighting we seek to focus on that reality.

Candle prayers can be used:

- At home as an evening devotion
- As an introduction to Morning or Evening Prayer
- At the start of a study group or Bible group
- As a means of affirming the day or night in the Lord's hands
- At the beginning of a Confirmation class or youth meeting
- At the lighting of the candles in church before the Eucharist
- The shorter part of each of the candle prayers, up to the prayer for candle lighting, can be used whenever we light a candle and also before saying grace at meals
- Each candle prayer can be used as a meditation in itself

Begin in the dark. If the room is not dark, close your eyes. Much of our life is spent in the dark and this is a symbol of our life without God, even though God is there in our darkness. You might like to affirm in the dark, 'The Lord is here', or use some positive words about the presence and power of God.

Now welcome the light, the light of God, into your life and your heart. You may like to give thanks for Jesus who is the Light of the World.

Use some words of Scripture, a poem or one or more of the suggested readings at this point to focus on why you have lit the candle at this time.

If you have any special intention, quietly lay this before God. During this time focus on the light and know that the light of God is with you and within you.

Relax in the light of God, concentrate on the light and allow God's light into your life. Let his light shine in your heart and in your eyes. Seek to know that the light of God is with us all; envisage that light surrounding each of your loved ones and all for whom you want to pray. Know that his presence is with them and his love is all about them. Pray that God's light may shine through you and reveal his light to others – that you may give out the light of God when the world around is in darkness. Seek God's blessing of light.

Finally, put the candle out. (Remember, leaving candles unattended can be dangerous.) At this point ask that you may take the light with you in your heart and mind.

The 'O Antiphons' are traditionally used in the last week of Advent leading up to Christmas Eve. These antiphons were usually sung or said at Vespers, or Evening Prayer, at the beginning and end of the Magnificat from 17 to the 23 December. They were usually sung to Gregorian chant, which is to plainsong. Each antiphon concentrates on a Scriptural title given to the coming Messiah, the Christ. So, all of the antiphons are about hope, expectation and the Promised One. One of the interesting things about the antiphons is that, if you read the first letter of each of them backwards they produce the Latin words 'ero cras' which translated means 'tomorrow I come'. The hymn 'O come, O come Emmanuel' is based on the 'O Antiphons' and in its fuller form is a lyrical rendition of the seven antiphons. A whole service can be built around the 'O Antiphons' using the relevant Scriptural readings and prayers. In the last week of Advent it is a good exercise to express your love for he who is the Light of the World by lighting a candle and reciting the relevant antiphon before a meal or in the evening at dusk when the lights are switched on. Though the antiphons are about the Coming One, we should also use them to come to him in love.

For the Advent season you may like to have special candles. The Advent candles are normally held together in an Advent wreath. To make an Advent wreath to hold the candles of Advent and Christmas is quite simple. First, obtain a circle of oasis from a florists and add greenery to it such as holly, ivy and yew (this reminds us we are dealing with eternal events). Now add four candles; some people like to use purple candles for Advent. In the centre of the circle add one larger white candle to represent Christ's arrival, 'God with us'. Advent is at the darkest time of the year, so it is good to bring a little light to it. The first week we will light one candle, the second two; by Christmas we will light all five. Then we will continue to light the five each week until Candlemas. We will need to replace any burnt-out candles with new ones. The burnt-out candles are symbols of those who have given their life to Christ and in the renewing of them we should offer our life to God. To make a simpler wreath use tea-lights on a tea plate with four around the outside and one in the centre; again, replace any that burn out. You can add a little greenery if you so wish.

In the same way, you can have a special candle for the Easter season. Easter candles can be bought from any church supplier, or you can just buy a transfer for a few pence and add it to a candle of your choice. However it is good for a family to make the Easter candle at home. If possible use a large and chunky candle as it will be lit for 50 days, from Easter Day to Pentecost, though from Ascension Day you may want it to look a little different. On the candle inscribe a cross. Do not do this too high up or will burn away too soon. At the head of the cross write the first letter of the Greek alphabet (alpha), A, and the last letter (omega), **Ω**, at the foot of the cross. You may like to inscribe the date below the omega. This reminds us of our Lord, who said: 'I am the Alpha and the Omega, the First and the Last, the Beginning and the End.' Now using five studs, or brass drawing pins, you could add the wounds of Christ; at the head of the cross for the crown of thorns, two on the arms of the cross for the nails that held his hands, one for the nail that held his feet, and one for the lance that pierced his side. Your Easter candle should look like this.

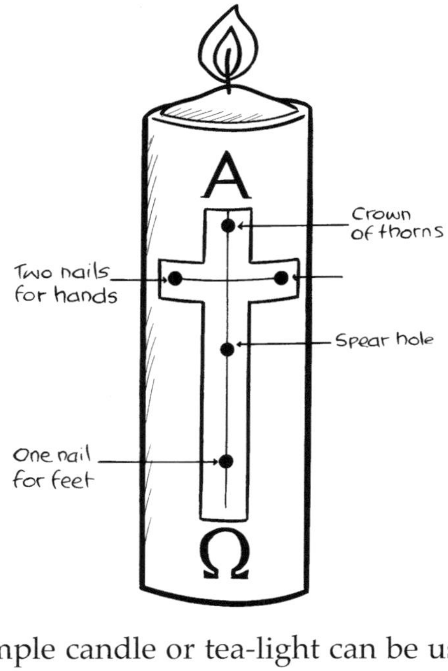

If you prefer, a simple candle or tea-light can be used. The important thing is to celebrate the triumph of our Lord over darkness and death, to rejoice that, in him, the Light of the World, life is eternal. At all times let the candle remind you of the power, the peace and above all the presence of our God.

Candle Prayers

Morning and evening prayer
Morning prayer 1

Begin in the dark. If the room is not dark, close your eyes. In the dark affirm the presence of God.

Welcome the light

By the tender mercy of our God,
the dawn from on high will break upon us,
to give light to those who sit in darkness,
and in the shadow of death,
to guide our feet into the way of peace.

Luke 1:78, 79

The Lord is here:
his spirit is with us

As we rejoice in the gift of this new day, may the light of your presence set our hearts on fire with love for you.

Common Worship, Morning Prayer

O God, Creator of light,
at the rising of your sun this morning,
let the greatest of all lights, your love,
rise like the sun within our hearts.

The Armenian Apostolic Church

Candle-lighting

Our God is the Light of the World:
a light that no darkness can quench.

The Light of Christ:
thanks be to God.

Light the candle.

Blessed are you, O Lord our God,
you are our light and salvation:
yours is the power, the glory, the splendour and the majesty,
now and always.
Open our ears to your call,
open our eyes to your light,
open our hearts to your love
that we may live to your praise and glory, now and always,
Father, Son and Holy Spirit.
Blessed be God for ever.

Special intention – in the light of God

We bring before you, O Lord,
the troubles and dangers of peoples and nations:
the sighing of prisoners and captives,
the sorrows of the bereaved,
the needs of strangers,
the helplessness of the weak,
the despondency of the weary,
the failing powers of the aged.
Upon all let your love and light shine,
for the sake of Christ the Light of the World.
Amen.

Adapted from prayer of St Anselm c.1033–1109

Closing prayer

Light of Jesus surround us.
Light of Jesus guide us.
Light of Jesus be within us.
Light of Jesus protect us.
Light of Jesus enfold us.
Light of Jesus transform us,
that we may be children of the Light
and walk in your Light.

Stay for a while rejoicing in the light of Christ.

Extinguish candle.

Morning prayer 2

Begin in the dark. If the room is not dark, close your eyes.

Welcome the light

Arise, shine; for your light is come, and the glory of the Lord is risen upon you. For darkness shall cover the earth, and thick darkness the peoples: but the glory of the Lord will rise upon you, and his glory will appear over you.

Isaiah 60:1, 2

We are in the light and love of the Lord:
Glory to the Father, Son and Holy Spirit.

O God, you brought us from the rest of night
to the light of this new day.
Bring us from the light this day
to the guiding light of eternity.

Traditional

Candle-lighting

Light of God shine upon us:
and scatter the darkness from within us and about us.

Light the candle.

Blessed are you Lord our God for you have called us out of darkness to be children of Light. The bright light of your presence scatters the darkness within us and is a lantern to our paths. Bless this light that it may remind us of your presence among us and of your love; through Christ our Lord.
Amen.

Light of God shining in our lives and throughout the world:
may we see and reflect the radiance of your glory.

Hymn

Christ, whose glory fills the skies

Special intention – in the light of God

Help us Lord:
to live in your light,
to act in your might,
to think in your wisdom,
to walk in your kingdom,
to abide in your love;
your presence to prove.
Amen.

Closing prayer

You encircle us, O God.
You surround us with your love.
You offer to us your light.
You enfold us in your peace.
You are with us this day and always.
You encircle us, O God.

Stay for a while rejoicing in the light of Christ.

Extinguish candle.

Evening prayer 1

Begin in the dark. If the room is not dark, close your eyes.

Welcome the light

The Lord, my God, lights up my darkness.
Psalm 18:28

Come, my Lord, my Light, my Way;
come, my lantern night and day;
come my healer, make me whole;
come my Saviour protect my soul;
come my King, enter my heart;
come Prince of Peace and never depart.
Come my King, enter my heart;
come Prince of Peace and never depart.

Candle-lighting

Our God is the Light of the World:
a light that no darkness can quench.

The Light of Christ:
thanks be to God.

Light the candle.

Blessed are you Lord God, Creator of all things,
you give life and light to the world.
As we light this candle to disperse the darkness
may the light of your love burn within our hearts.
Blessed are you Father, Son and Holy Spirit.

Reading

The Lord is my light and my salvation; whom shall I fear?
The Lord is my light and my salvation.

The Lord is the stronghold of my life; of whom shall I be afraid?
The Lord is my light and my salvation.

Glory be to the Father, and to the Son, and to the Holy Spirit.
The Lord is my light and my salvation.

Psalm 27:1, 2

Special intention – in the light of God

Pray for all whom you have met this day,
those you have worked with,
those you live with
and all who need your prayers.

Watch, thou dear Lord,
with those who wake, or watch, or weep tonight,
and give your angels charge over those who sleep.
Tend your sick ones, Lord Christ,
rest your weary ones,
bless your dying ones,
soothe your suffering ones,
pity your afflicted ones,
shield your joyous ones.
I ask all this for your love's sake.

St Augustine of Hippo 354 – 430

Closing prayer

God in the night,
God at my right,
God all the day,
God with me stay,
God in my heart
never depart.
God with thy might
keep us in light
through this dark night.

Extinguish candle.

Evening prayer 2

Begin in the dark. If the room is not dark, close your eyes.

Welcome the light

The presence, the power and the protection of God are with us and about us. We are in the Light of the Father, the Son and the Holy Spirit.

Candle-lighting

Our God is the Light of the World:
a light that no darkness can quench.

The Light of Christ:
thanks be to God.

Light the candle.

Blessed are you, Lord our God, you give us life and you continually renew and refresh us with your presence and your love. You are the strength of the weak and the light to all who walk in darkness. Blessed are you Father, Son and Holy Spirit.

I come in weakness to the power of God.
God is my salvation; I will trust and not be afraid, for the Lord is my strength and my might; and has become my salvation.

Isaiah 12:2

I come in darkness to the light of God.
God is my salvation; I will trust and not be afraid, for the Lord is my strength and my might; and has become my salvation.

I come in fear to the peace of God.
God is my salvation; I will trust and not be afraid, for the Lord is my strength and my might; and has become my salvation.

I come with troubles to the healing of God.
God is my salvation; I will trust and not be afraid, for the Lord is my strength and my might; and has become my salvation.

I come in need to the love of God.
God is my salvation; I will trust and not be afraid, for the Lord is my strength and my might; and has become my salvation.

Hymn

O gracious light, Lord Jesus Christ

Special intention – in the light of God

Eternal Light, shine in our hearts:
Eternal Goodness, deliver us from evil;
Eternal Power, be our support;
Eternal Wisdom, scatter the darkness of our ignorance;
Eternal Pity, have mercy upon us;
that with all our heart and mind and soul and strength
we may seek your face
and be brought by your infinite mercy
to your Holy Presence;
through Jesus Christ our Lord.
Amen.

Alcuin of York 735–804

Closing prayer

Holy God, Holy and Strong One,
conquer the darkness within us and about us:
let your blessing rest upon us,
upon our homes and our loved ones,
that we may abide in your peace,
in your presence and in your light,
now and for evermore.
Amen.

Extinguish candle.

Advent 1
God's faithful people

Advent is a time when we rejoice in the coming of Christ into our lives, that he came at Christmas, and that he comes again to be our Lord and King. Advent celebrates that our God comes to us again and again.

Begin in the dark. If the room is not dark, close your eyes.

Welcome the light

The people who walked in darkness have seen a great light; they who lived in a land of deep darkness, on them the light has shined.

Isaiah 9:2

Candle-lighting

On the first Sunday in Advent we light one candle to say with all faithful people:

The Lord comes to us.
He abides with us.

When our lives are darkened it is necessary to celebrate God's presence that comes to us and the light that God gives us.

Light one Advent candle.

Jesus Christ is the Light of the World:
Eternal Light, shine in our hearts.

Blessed are you, Lord our God, for you have called us out of darkness to be children of Light. The bright light of your presence scatters the darkness within us and is a lantern to our paths. Bless this light, that

it may remind us of your presence among us and your love towards us; through Christ our Lord.
Amen.

Reading

Genesis 18:1–15

Hymn

The God of Abraham praise *(Third verse)*

Special intention – in the light of God

When this world is as dark as night,
you are the one we call the Light.
Come, Lord Jesus.

When we are tempted to go astray,
you are the one we call the Way.
Come, Lord Jesus.

When the storms of life increase,
you are the one we call our Peace.
Come, Lord Jesus.

When troubles to our lives bring harm,
you are the one who brings us calm.
Come, Lord Jesus.

Almighty God, give us grace to cast away the works of darkness and to put on the armour of light, now in the time of this mortal life, in which your Son Jesus Christ came to us in great humility; so that on the last day, when he shall come again in His glorious majesty to judge the living and the dead, we may rise to the life immortal; through Him who is alive and reigns with you and the Holy Spirit, one God, now and for ever.
Amen.

Common Worship Collect for Advent I

Closing prayer

Lord of Life, of Light, of Love,
come that I may fully live;
come that I may walk in the light;
come that I may burn with your love.
Come Lord this day, I welcome you.

Extinguish candle.

Advent 2
Men and women of vision

Advent is a time when we rejoice in the coming of Christ into our lives, that he came at Christmas, and that he comes again to be our Lord and King. Advent celebrates that our God comes to us again and again.

Begin in the dark. If the room is not dark, close your eyes.

Welcome the light

Your word is a lamp to my feet and a light to my path.

Psalm 119:105

Lord, open our eyes to your presence.
Come, Lord of light.

Lord, open our ears to your call.
Come, Lord of light.

Lord, open our hearts to your love.
Come, Lord of light.

Lord, open our lives to your guiding.
Come, Lord of light.

Candle-lighting

On the second Sunday in Advent we light two candles, one for all of God's faithful people and one for men and women of vision. When our lives are darkened it is necessary to celebrate the presence that comes to us and the vision that is given to us.

The Lord comes to us.
He abides with us.

Light two Advent candles.

Jesus Christ is the Light of the World:
eternal light, shine in our hearts.

Blessed are you, Lord God, for you open the eyes of blind. You gave vision and insight to the prophets. We thank you for Amos and Hosea, for Isaiah, Jeremiah and Ezekiel and all the prophets, and for all people who have extended our awareness through their vision. You are their God and our God, their Father and our Father. Help us to know that as you came to them you come to us.
Blessed be God for ever.

Reading

Isaiah 6:1–8

Hymn

Be thou my vision *(First verse)*

Special intention – in the light of God

Holy God, holy and Strong One,
guide us to do what you would have us do;
inspire us to be the people you would have us be.
Lord, deliver us from lack of vision,
keep us from dullness of sight.
Help us to be true to you and ourselves
that we may live with integrity.
You give, O Lord, purpose to our days
and a meaning to our lives.
May we live to your glory
and for the good of this world.
Amen.

Closing prayer

Open my eyes, Lord, that I may see
your presence is ever with me.
Open my ears, Lord, to hear your voice
and in your will may I rejoice.
Open my heart, Lord, to your great heart
and from your love may I never depart.

Extinguish candles.

Advent 3
John the Baptist

Advent is a time when we rejoice in the coming of Christ into our lives, that he came at Christmas, and that he comes again to be our Lord and King. Advent celebrates that our God comes to us again and again.

Begin in the dark. If the room is not dark, close your eyes.

Welcome the light

It is you who light my lamp; the Lord my God lights up my darkness.
Psalm 18:28

Rejoice, for the Lord is at hand.
Our God comes to us to give us his joy and peace.
To give us hope in our world,
hope in our hearts,
hope in our homes,
hope in our lives.
God, we rejoice at your coming
and pray that your kingdom comes in us today.

Candle-lighting

On the third Sunday in Advent we light three candles, one for all of God's faithful people, one for men and women of vision, and one for John the Baptist and all who immerse themselves in the love and presence of God.

When our lives are darkened it is necessary to celebrate the presence that comes to us and the light that is given to us.

The Lord comes to us.
He abides with us.

Light three Advent candles.

Jesus Christ is the Light of the World:
Eternal Light, shine in our hearts.

Blessed are you, Lord our God, for you sent your messenger John the Baptist to prepare the way and make ready for your coming; grant that we may be prepared and ready to receive and welcome you into our lives and homes. As you come to us in love may we abide in your love and in your presence this day and for ever. Blessed be God, Father, Son and Holy Spirit.
Blessed be God for ever.

Reading

Matthew 3:1–6

Hymn

Hark! a thrilling voice is sounding

Special intention – in the light of God

Loving God, as we give you thanks for John the Baptist,
may all peoples know they are immersed in your presence.
Bless all preachers of the word
that they may reveal that your kingdom is at hand.
Give us, O Lord, the courage to seek your will
and to strive to forward your kingdom on earth.
As your faithful people prepare for Christmas,
may they welcome you into their hearts and homes.

Closing prayer

Father, you created us by your love and for your love.
May we abide in you and you in us.

Jesus, you redeemed us by your love and for your love.
May we abide in you and you in us.

Spirit of God, you guide us by your love and for your love.
May we abide in you and you in us.

Holy and Blessed Three, your love enfolds and surrounds us.
May we abide in you and you in us.

Extinguish candles.

Advent 4
The Blessed Virgin Mary

Advent is a time when we rejoice in the coming of Christ into our lives, that he came at Christmas, and that he comes again to be our Lord and King. Advent celebrates that our God comes to us again and again.

Begin in the dark. If the room is not dark, close your eyes.

Welcome the light

In him was life, and the life was the light of all people. The light shines in the darkness, and the darkness did not overcome it.

John 1:4, 5

In Christ Jesus the darkness is defeated:
his light has come into the world.
Emmanuel, God is with us.

In Christ Jesus a new day has dawned:
his light has come into the world.
Emmanuel, God is with us.

In Christ Jesus is our hope and joy:
his light has come into the world.
Emmanuel, God is with us.

In Christ Jesus life is eternal:
his light has come into the world.
Emmanuel, God is with us.

Candle-lighting

On the fourth Sunday in Advent we light four candles, one for all of God's faithful people, one for men and women of vision, and one for

John the Baptist and all who immerse themselves in the love and presence of God. The fourth candle is for the Blessed Virgin Mary and all who give themselves to God in love.

When our lives are darkened it is necessary to celebrate the presence that comes to us and the light that is given to us.

The Lord comes to us.
He abides with us.

Light four Advent candles.

Jesus Christ is the Light of the World;
eternal light, shine in our hearts.

Blessed are you, Lord our God, for in the fullness of time you shared in our humanity, being born of the Blessed Virgin Mary. You came down to lift us up; you became human that we might share in the divine. As we rejoice in Mary doing your will and so welcoming you into her life may we abide in you and know that you abide in us. Blessed are you Father, Son and Holy Spirit.
Blessed be God for ever.

Reading

Isaiah 7:10–14

Hymn

Hark the glad sound

Special intention – in the light of God

We bring before you, O Lord,
all whose lives are darkened.
We remember the poor and the homeless,
all who are ill and suffering,
those who are approaching death,
and all who have lost loved ones.

Lord be known to them, come as the light,
let your peace fill them and your love enfold them.
We ask this for you love and mercy's sake.
Amen.

Closing prayer

O Light that lightens our way,
let us not fear the darkness of this day.
To open to you is to welcome the Light.
To walk in your light is to know eternal life.
Come, Lord Jesus, be known to all who walk in darkness.
Come, Lord Jesus, you are our light and our salvation.
Come, Lord of life.

Extinguish candles.

17 December

O Sapientia
The wisdom of God

Begin in the dark. If the room is not dark, close your eyes.

Welcome the light

O Wisdom coming out from the Most High, filling all creation and reigning to the ends of the earth: come and teach us the way of truth.
Amen.
Come, Lord Jesus.

Candle-lighting

He is the source of your life in Christ Jesus, who became for us wisdom from God, and righteousness and sanctification and redemption.

1 Corinthians 1:30

Come, Lord, with your grace and goodness:
come to our hearts and change us.
Come, wisdom of God.
Come, Christ our Lord.

Come, Lord, with your peace and power:
come to our lives and strengthen us.
Come, wisdom of God.
Come, Christ our Lord.

Come, Lord, with your light and love:
come to our darkness and enlighten us.
Come, wisdom of God.
Come, Christ our Lord.

Jesus Christ, the wisdom of God, is the Light of the World.
A light that no darkness can quench.

Light the candle.

Blessed are you, Lord our God, for in your wisdom you have created us and by your wisdom you have redeemed us. Blessed are you Father, Son and Holy Spirit.
Blessed be God for ever.

Reading

Proverbs 2:1–15

Hymn

O come, O come, Emmanuel *(Second verse and refrain)*

Special intention – in the light of God

O wisdom, issuing out of the mouth of God;
maranatha.
Come, Lord Jesus.

O wisdom, the very breath and power of God;
maranatha.
Come, Lord Jesus.

O wisdom, the image and goodness of God;
maranatha.
Come, Lord Jesus.

O wisdom, passing into holy souls;
maranatha.
Come, Lord Jesus.

O wisdom, working in the prophets;
maranatha.
Come, Lord Jesus.

O wisdom, triumphing over evil;
maranatha.
Come, Lord Jesus.

O wisdom, dancing in creation;
maranatha.
Come, Lord Jesus.

Closing prayer

God, give us grace to accept with serenity
the things that cannot be changed,
the courage to change the things that should be changed,
and the wisdom to know the difference.

Reinhold Niebuhr 1892–1971

O Wisdom, coming out from the Most High, filling all creation and reigning to the ends of the earth: come and teach us the way of truth.
Amen.
Come, Lord Jesus.

May the Lord when he comes find us watching and waiting.

Extinguish candle.

18 December

O Adonai
The Lord of lords

Begin in the dark. If the room is not dark, close your eyes.

Welcome the light

O Lord of lords and leader of the house of Israel, you appeared to Moses in the fire of the burning bush and gave your law on Sinai; come and save us with your mighty arm and redeem us.
Amen.
Come, Lord Jesus.

Lord of the burning bush,
scatter our darkness and make yourself known to us;
maranatha.
Come, Lord Jesus.

Lord of the desert,
lead us to the waters of life;
maranatha.
Come, Lord Jesus.

Lord of the Rock,
shelter us and protect us;
maranatha.
Come, Lord Jesus.

Lord of the living water,
refresh and restore us;
maranatha.
Come, Lord Jesus.

Lord of the manna,
strengthen and sustain us;
maranatha.
Come, Lord Jesus.

Lord of Mount Sinai,
Direct and guide us;
maranatha.
Come, Lord Jesus.

Lord, our Friend and Saviour,
redeem us and bring us to the Promised Land;
maranatha.
Come, Lord Jesus.

Candle-lighting

Jesus Christ our Lord is the Light of the World.
A light no darkness can put out.

Light the candle.

Blessed are you, Lord God Almighty, for you have revealed your presence to us through prophets, saints and holy people. As you made yourself known to Moses may we know that you are with us and abide with us in our journeying. Blessed are you, Father, Son and Holy Spirit.
Blessed be God for ever.

Reading

Exodus 3:1–6

Hymn

O come, O come, Emmanuel *(Third verse and refrain)*

Special intention – in the light of God

Lord, teach us and all peoples to live by your law of love.
Guide us in our journeying through life;
strengthen and sustain all who are struggling;
shield and shelter us until we enter the fullness of your kingdom.
We ask this in the love of our Lord, Jesus Christ.
Amen.

Closing prayer

The leading of the Lord go before us.
The light of the Lord be about us.
The love of the Lord enfold us.
Now and for evermore.

O Lord of lords and leader of the house of Israel, you appeared to Moses in the fire of the burning bush and gave your law on Sinai; come and save us with your mighty arm and redeem us.
Amen.
Come, Lord Jesus.

May the Lord when he comes find us watching and waiting.

Extinguish candle.

19 December

O Radix Jesse
The Root of Jesse

Begin in the dark. If the room is not dark, close your eyes.

Welcome the light

O Root of Jesse, standing as a sign among the nations: kings will keep silence before you for whom the nations long: come and save us and delay no longer.
Amen.
Come Lord, Jesus.

Blessed be the Lord the God of Israel,
who has come to his people and set them free.
Blessed be the Lord the God of Israel.

He has raised up for us a mighty Saviour,
born of the house of his servant David.
Blessed be the Lord the God of Israel.

Glory be to the Father, the Son, and the Holy Spirit.
Blessed be the Lord the God of Israel.

Benedictus from Luke 1:68–69

Candle lighting

Jesus Christ is the Light of the World.
A light that no darkness can extinguish.

Light the candle.

Blessed are you Lord God, King of Glory,
revealed in the face of our Lord Jesus Christ;
revealed in him who is born of the house of David:
revealed in the Light that scatters our darkness;
revealed in him that is the hope of all the world.
Blessed are you, Lord our God, now and for ever.

Reading

Isaiah 11:1–4a, 6–10

Hymn

O come, O come Emmanuel *(Fourth verse and refrain)*

Special intention – in the light of God

Jesus, Word made flesh;
maranatha.
Come, Lord, dwell among us.

Jesus, born of the house of David:
maranatha.
Come, Lord, dwell among us.

Jesus, born of the blessed Virgin Mary;
maranatha.
Come, Lord, dwell among us.

Jesus, sharing in our humanity;
maranatha.
Come, Lord, dwell among us.

Closing prayer

Jesus, born of Mary, bless all parents in their care for their children.
Jesus, born in a stable, be a strength to all who are homeless.
Jesus, taken into Egypt, be known among the refugees and migrants.

Jesus, sharing in our humanity, bring us to know the mystery of your divinity.
Jesus, King of Glory, help us to know you are with us now and always.
O root of Jesse, standing as a sign among the nations: kings will keep silence before you for whom the nations long. Come and save us and delay no longer.
Amen.
Come Lord, Jesus.

May the Lord when he comes find us watching and waiting.

Extinguish candle.

20 December

O Clavis David
The Key of David

Begin in the dark. If the room is not dark, close your eyes.

Welcome the light

O Key of David and sceptre of the House of Israel; you open and none can shut; you shut and none can open. Come, free the captives from prison, and break down the walls of death.
Amen.
Come, Lord Jesus.

O Key of David,
you open to us your love.
Come, Lord,
be known among us.

O Key of David,
you come to set the prisoner free
Come, Lord,
be known among us.

O Key of David,
you open to us the kingdom of heaven.
Come, Lord,
be known among us.

O Key of David,
you open to us eternal life.
Come, Lord,
be known among us.

Candle-lighting

Jesus Christ is the Light of the World.
A light that no darkness can extinguish.

Light the candle.

Blessed are you, Lord our God, for in your grace and goodness you sent your Son into the world and he has opened for us the kingdom of heaven. We give you thanks for every opportunity you set before us to know and love you. Open our eyes to your presence and our hearts to your love. Blessed are you Father, Son and Holy Spirit.
Blessed be God for ever.

Reading

Revelation 3:7; 5:2–5

Hymn

O come, O come, Emmanuel *(Fifth verse and refrain)*

Special intention – in the light of God

Christ, Key of David, we bring before you
all who are locked in on themselves:
we bring all prisoners,
all who are bound by addiction,
all who are held by vice,
all who are captives to habit,
all who are restricted by their environment,
all who suffer from tyranny,
all who feel trapped by life.
Jesus, we come to you, our Redeemer,
for in your love you seek to release those who are bound.

Closing prayer

Loving Lord,
open our eyes to your presence,
open our ears to your call,
open our hearts to your love.

O Key of David and sceptre of the House of Israel; you open and none can shut; you shut and none can open: come, free the captives from prison, and break down the walls of death.
Amen.
Come, Lord Jesus.

May the Lord when he comes find us watching and waiting.

Extinguish candle.

21 December

O Oriens
Christ the Morning Star

Begin in the dark. If the room is not dark, close your eyes.

Welcome the light

O morning star, splendour of the light eternal and bright sun of righteousness: come with your light to all who dwell in darkness and in the shadow of death.
Amen.
Come, Lord Jesus.

Arise and shine; for your light has come,
the glory of the Lord has risen upon you.
Arise and shine for your light has come.

For darkness shall cover the earth,
and thick darkness the peoples.
Arise and shine for your light has come.

But the Lord will arise upon you,
and his glory will appear over you.
Arise and shine for your light has come.

Nations shall come to your light
and kings to the brightness of your dawn.
Arise and shine for your light has come.

Glory be to the Father, and to the Son, and to the Holy Spirit.
Arise and shine for your light has come.

Isaiah 60:1–3

Christ is the Morning Star,
who, when the night of this world is past,
brings to his saints the promise of the light
of life and opens everlasting day.

Bede 671–735

Candle-lighting

Blessed are you, Lord our God, Creator of light out of darkness.
In this season of Advent, when the sun's light is swallowed up,
by the increasing darkness of night,
you offer us the splendour of your glory, revealed in Christ our Morning Star.
Through him you call us to be children of the day and not of the night, and to walk in the presence of he who is the Light of the World, even Christ our Lord.
Blessed are you Father, Son and Holy Spirit.
Blessed be God for ever.

Light the candle.

Readings

Psalm 107:10–14; Luke 1:78, 79; Revelation 22:16

Hymn

O come, O come, Emmanuel *(Sixth verse and refrain)*

Special intention – in the light of God

Christ as a light illumine and guide me,
Christ as shield overshadow me,
Christ be under me, Christ be over me,
Christ beside me, on my left and my right.
This day be within and without me;
lowly and meek, yet all-powerful.

Be to the heart of each one to whom I speak;
in the mouth of each who speaks unto me;
lowly and meek, yet all powerful.
Christ as a light, Christ as shield,
Christ beside me on my left and my right.

Attributed to St Patrick

Closing prayer

O Christ, our Morning Star,
Splendour of Light Eternal,
shining with the glory of the rainbow,
come and waken us,
from the greyness of our apathy
and renew us with your gift of hope.

Bede 671–735

O Morning Star, splendour of the light eternal and bright sun of righteousness: come with your light to all who dwell in darkness and in the shadow of death.
Amen.
Come, Lord Jesus.

May the Lord when he comes find us watching and waiting.

Extinguish candle.

22 December

O Rex Gentium
King of the nations

Begin in the dark. If the room is not dark, close your eyes.

Welcome the light

O King of the nations, you alone can fulfil their desires: Cornerstone; binding all together, come and save the creature you have fashioned from the earth.
Amen.
Come, Lord Jesus.

Great and amazing are your deeds, Lord God the Almighty.
We watch for you, we wait for you.

Just and true are your ways, O King of the nations!
We watch for you, we wait for you.

Lord, who will not fear and glorify your name?
For you alone are holy.
We watch for you, we wait for you.

All nations shall come and worship before you,
for your judgements have been revealed.
We watch for you, we wait for you.

Revelation 15:3b, 4

Candle-lighting

Jesus Christ is the Light of the World.
A light that no darkness can extinguish.

Light the candle.

Blessed are you, Lord our God, for you have created all things.
You created us out of love and for your love.
You sent your Son to be our Saviour.
He lived among us and faced death that we might know eternal life.
Now he is the King of kings and Lord of lords
and in seeking to do his will we are one with him in his kingdom.
We look for the time when the kingdoms of the world
will become the kingdom of Christ our Lord.
Blessed are you Father, Son and Holy Spirit.
Blessed be God for ever.

Reading

Jeremiah 30:7–11a; Acts 4:10–12

Hymn

O come, O come, Emmanuel *(Seventh verse and refrain)*

Special intention – in the light of God

Come to your world, O King of the nations.
We look for you: we long for you.

Christ our King, let your word be a light to our feet, a lantern to our path.
We look for you: we long for you.

Christ our King, come and rule in our hearts.
We look for you: we long for you.

Christ our King, come, be known to all people in all places.
We look for you: we long for you.

Come, that the kingdoms of the world may become the kingdom of Christ.
We look for you: we long for you.

Closing prayer

Lord, your kingdom come as in heaven.
Come in my heart, Lord,
come in my actions,
come in my mind,
come in my whole life,
come, High King of heaven.
For in your coming heaven and earth become one.
Lord, your kingdom come as in heaven.

O King of the nations, you alone can fulfil their desires: Cornerstone; binding all together, come and save the creature you have fashioned from the earth.
Amen.
Come, Lord Jesus.

May the Lord when he comes find us watching and waiting.

Extinguish candle.

23 December

O Emmanuel

Begin in the dark. If the room is not dark, close your eyes.

Welcome the light

O Emmanuel, our King and our Lawgiver, hope of the nations and their Saviour: come and save us, O Lord our God.
Amen.
Come, Lord Jesus.

O Emmanuel, God with us,
open our eyes to your presence.
Come, Lord Jesus.

Make our homes your home.
Come, Lord Jesus.

Make room in our lives for you.
Come, Lord Jesus.

O Emmanuel, God ever present,
reveal your self to us.
Come, Lord Jesus.

Candle-lighting

Jesus Christ is the Light of the World.
A light that no darkness can quench.

Light the candle.

Reading

Matthew 1:18–23

Hymn

O come, O come, Emmanuel *(First verse and refrain)*

Special intention – in the light of God

Our Lord says, 'Surely I am coming quickly.' Even so come, Lord Jesus.
Come, dwell among us.

O Wisdom, filling all of creation, come and make us friends of God.
Come, dwell among us.

O Lord of lords, who appeared to Moses in the burning bush,
come and make yourself known to us.
Come, dwell among us.

O Root of Jesse, taking upon you our humanity that we may share in your divinity,
come, dwell among us.

Key of David, when you open no one can close; come bring us to the glorious liberty of the children of God.
Come, dwell among us.

O Morning Star, Splendour of eternal light,
come give light to all who walk in darkness and in the shadow of death.
Come, dwell among us.

O King of the nations, ruler we long for, come in love and peace to save your people.
Come, dwell among us.

O Emmanuel, God ever present, make yourself known to us.
Come, dwell among us.

Closing prayer

O Emmanuel, our King and our Lawgiver, hope of the nations and their Saviour: come and save us, O Lord our God.
Amen.
Come, Lord Jesus.

May the Lord when he comes find us watching and waiting.

Extinguish candle.

Christmas Eve

Begin in the dark. If the room is not dark, close your eyes.

Welcome the light

What has come into being in him was life, and the life was the light of all people. The light shines in the darkness and the darkness has not overcome it.

John 1:4, 5

The Eternal Word, born of the Father before time began, today emptied himself for our sake and became one of us.

Evening Prayer, Christmas Eve

This holy night, the darkness is scattered,
for the King of Glory comes to dwell among us.
This holy night Christ comes to earth;
in him heaven and earth are one.
This holy night we join the angels in praise
singing, 'Glory to God on high and on earth peace.'
This holy night let us join with the shepherds
and come and kneel before the Christ child.

Candle-lighting

Jesus Christ is the Light of the World.
The light that no darkness can quench.

The Light of Christ.
Thanks be to God.

Light the candle.

Blessed is Jesus, the Lord our Saviour:
blessed is he who shared our humanity,
that we might partake of his divinity.
Blessed is he who became a mortal that we might know eternal life.
Blessed is he who became poor to enrich us all.
Blessed is he who fulfilled the dreams and visions of the prophets.
Blessed is he who is the Babe of Bethlehem yet King of kings
and Lord of lords.
Blessed is Jesus, the Lord our Saviour.

O God, who made this most hallowed night
resplendent with the glory of the true Light,
grant that we who have known the mystery of that Light on earth,
may enter into the fullness of his joys in heaven.

Ancient Western Rite

Reading

Luke 2:8–20

Hymn

In the bleak midwinter *(Final verse)*

Special intention – in the light of God

Lord Jesus, babe of Bethlehem,
we ask your blessing upon all newborn children.
Lord Jesus, born in a stable,
give hope and courage to all who are homeless and poor.
Lord Jesus, soon to become a refugee because of Herod,
give strength to all who are persecuted and who suffer from violence.
Lord Jesus, King of Glory, with the angels and shepherds,
we adore you and rejoice in your coming among us.
Lord Jesus, as you came out of love for us,
we seek to give our love and our lives to you.

Closing prayer

This holy night you, Lord, come down and dwell among us.
Heaven and earth are one in you.
God and our humanity are united.
The heavenly glory is seen in human flesh.
Darkness is conquered by the Light of the World.
You, Lord, are one with us.
May we go on our way rejoicing.

Extinguish candle.

Christmas Day

Begin in the dark. If the room is not dark, close your eyes.

Welcome the light

The Word became flesh and lived among us, and we have seen his glory, the glory as of a father's only son, full of grace and truth.

John 1:14

The following affirmation can be used while four Advent candles are lit or simply as a rejoicing before the lighting of the Christ Candle.

The Christ is come into the world. Emmanuel,
the Lord is with us. Amen.

Jesus is born among us. Emmanuel,
the Lord is with us. Amen.

Our God has taken upon him our flesh. Emmanuel,
the Lord is with us. Amen.

This is the light that defeats the darkness. Emmanuel,
the Lord is with us. Amen.

Candle-lighting

Today the Saviour, promised long, is come. Emmanuel,
the Lord is with us. Amen.

The Saviour comes among us and is here. Emmanuel,
the Lord is with us. Amen.

His light shines in darkness that is about us.
(Light the Christ candle.)
Emmanuel,
the Lord is with us. Amen.

Blessed are you, Lord our God,
for in your deep love for us
you have shared in our humanity
that we might share in your glory.
Help us to make room in our lives for you each day.
Let us be aware of you and of your coming to us.
May we know that we live in you as you live in us.
Blessed are you Father, Son and Holy Spirit.

Reading

Luke 2:1–14 or John 1:1–14

Hymn

Hark, the herald-angels sing *(First verse and refrain)*

Special intention – in the light of God

May we make room with the innkeeper
and know the joy of the shepherds,
the message of the angels,
the seeking of the wise men,
the bliss of Mary,
the presence of the Christ-child:
and may we rejoice in the Word made flesh
dwelling among us.

Closing prayer

O holy Child of Bethlehem,
descend to us we pray,
cast out our sin, and enter in;
be born in us today.

Extinguish candle.

Epiphany
The wise men

Begin in the dark. If the room is not dark, close your eyes.

Welcome the light

The people who walked in darkness have seen a great light; they who lived in a land of deep darkness, on them the light has shined.

Isaiah 9:2

Jesus, Word made flesh dwelling among us,
come, lighten our darkness.

Jesus, born of the Blessed Virgin Mary,
come, lighten our darkness.

Jesus, adored by the wise men,
come, lighten our darkness.

Jesus, revealed to the world,
come, lighten our darkness.

Candle-lighting

Jesus here and with us now,
come, lighten our darkness.

Jesus Christ is the Light of the World.
A light that no darkness can extinguish.

Light the candle.

Blessed are you, O Lord God, who by the leading of a star brought the wise men to come before Jesus. Through him, who is our Saviour, you reveal your love and light to the whole world. In our seeking, guide us that we may come before you, that we may come to know you, to love you and to worship you this day and always. Blessed are you Father, Son and Holy Spirit.

Lord God, to live without you is to walk in the darkness:
to live in awareness of you is to live in the light.
Help us to know and to reveal your love
and your light through Jesus Christ our Lord.
Amen.

Reading

Matthew 2:1–12

Hymn

As with gladness men of old *(First verse)*

Special intention – in the light of God

Blessed be God, who by the leading of a star brought the wise men to Christ the King.
The Word has become flesh
and now lives among us.

Blessed be God, who is the God of all the nations.
The Word has become flesh
and now lives among us.

Blessed be God, who comes to all peoples, in all places and all the time.
The Word has become flesh
and now lives among us.

Christ was proclaimed by the angels.
The Word has become flesh
and now lives among us.

Christ was worshipped by the shepherds.
The Word has become flesh
and now lives among us.

Christ was adored by the wise men.
The Word has become flesh
and now lives among us.

Christ is worshipped throughout the world.
The Word has become flesh
and now lives among us.

Closing prayer

Lord, we come to the light of your presence and to your love.
Lord, whom we sought in the sky, you are found here among us.
Lord, who remained long hidden from sight,
you are found in an infant.
Today we rejoice, for heaven has come to earth:
earth is taken up into heaven.
God is found in human flesh and our humanity is taken up into God.
He whom the universe could not contain is found in a tiny child.
We come and adore with those who seek you.
We acknowledge you as our King and our God.
We know you have shared in our sorrows to redeem us.
We offer ourselves to you who came down to raise us up.
We adore you, Christ our Lord.

Extinguish candle.

Candle Prayers

Epiphany
The water made wine

Begin in the dark. If the room is not dark, close your eyes.

Welcome the light

Today we celebrate the first miracle of Jesus at the wedding feast in Cana when he turned the water into wine. We celebrate the revealing of the power of Jesus to change our lives. We rejoice in Christ's power to transform us and to fill our emptiness with the riches of his glory.
The Lord is here:
his Spirit is with us.

He gives power to the faint, and strengthens the powerless. Those who wait on the Lord shall renew their strength, they shall mount up with wings like eagles, they shall run and not be weary, they shall walk and not faint.

Isaiah 40:29, 31

Lord, you know our needs before we ask and are always more ready to give than we desire or deserve. We come to you for healing, for renewal and for the fullness of life eternal.
Amen.

Candle-lighting

Jesus Christ is the Light of the world.
A light that no darkness can extinguish.

Light the candle.

Blessed are you, Lord our God; you have made us in your image, and restored that image through your Son, Christ our Lord. You fill our emptiness with your presence, you transform our weakness by your power, you make what is common into that which is precious.

As Christ changed the water into wine, you renew our lives each day.
Blessed are you Father, Son and Holy Spirit.

Reading

John 2:1–11

Hymn

New every morning is the love

Special intention – in the light of God

Holy God, holy and Strong One, in our emptiness we come to be filled by you.
The Lord is my light and my salvation.

Holy God, holy and Strong One, in our darkness we come to your light.
The Lord is my light and my salvation.

Holy God, holy and Strong One, in our troubles we come to your love.
The Lord is my light and my salvation.

Holy God, holy and Strong One, in illness we come for your healing.
The Lord is my light and my salvation.

Holy God, holy and Strong One, in need we come to your salvation.
The Lord is my light and my salvation.

Closing prayer

Lord, at the wedding of Cana,
you transformed common water into wine –
come and change us, that we may know you and your love:
as you, dear Lord, have taken on our humanity
may we now partake of your Divinity.
Good Lord, transform us that we may reveal your glory.

Extinguish candle.

Epiphany
Sharing in the mission of Christ

Begin in the dark. If the room is not dark, close your eyes.

Welcome the light

Arise, shine, for your light has come, and the glory of the Lord is risen upon you. For darkness shall cover the earth, and thick darkness the peoples; but the glory of the Lord will arise upon you, and his glory will appear over you. Nations shall come to you light, and kings to the brightness of your dawn.

Isaiah 60:1–3

The light which the wise men followed was found in the Christ child.
The Lord is our light and our salvation.

Candle-lighting

Jesus Christ is the Light of the world.
A light that no darkness can extinguish.

Light the candle.

Blessed are you, Lord our God, for you have called us to know you and to walk in your light. You have called us to love you and to reveal your light in our lives and to the world. Blessed are you, Father, Son and Holy Spirit, for you have called us into life and life eternal. Blessed be God for ever.

Readings

Matthew 28:16–20; Matthew 5:14–16

Hymn

I, the Lord of sea and sky

Set our hearts on fire with love for you, O Christ,
that in its flame we may love you,
with all our heart,
with all our mind,

with all our soul,
and with all our strength,
and our neighbour as ourselves,
so that, in keeping your commandments,
we may glorify you, the giver of all good gifts.

Kontakion for Love, Eastern Orthodox Church

Special intention – in the light of God

In your coming, O Christ, the darkness is conquered.
Jesus, Light of the World, I give myself to you.

You Lord, in your light, reveal to us your love.
Jesus, Light of the World, I give myself to you.

You, Lord, are the Light to lighten all the nations.
Jesus, Light of the World, I give myself to you.

You, Lord, ask us to let our light shine in the world.
Jesus, Light of the World, I give myself to you.

You, Lord, have called us to witness to you.
Jesus, Light of the World, I give myself to you.

May the world know that we dwell in you and you in us.

Closing prayer

Arise, shine; for your light has come,
and the glory of the Lord has risen upon you.
Arise, shine; for your light has come.

For darkness shall cover the earth, and thick darkness the peoples;
but the Lord will arise upon you, and his glory will appear over you.
Arise, shine; for your light has come.

Nations shall come to your light, and kings to the brightness of your dawn.
Arise, shine; for your light has come.

Extinguish candle.

Epiphany
The baptism of our Lord

Today you might like to renew your baptismal vows and say the creed.

Begin in the dark. If the room is not dark, close your eyes.

Welcome the light

In those days Jesus came from Nazareth of Galilee and was baptised by John in the Jordan.

Mark 1:9

We give thanks for the baptism of Jesus by John in the river Jordan. We rejoice that God's voice was heard affirming his Son and that the Holy Spirit was known to descend upon Jesus. Rejoice, for we are always immersed in the presence of God, Father, Son and Holy Spirit. We abide in him as he abides in us. In the name of the Father, and of the Son and of the Holy Spirit.
Amen.

The Lord is here:
his Spirit is with us.

Candle-lighting

Jesus Christ is the Light of the World.
A light that no darkness can extinguish.

Light the candle.

O Lord Jesus, you came down to dwell among us,
you were fully immersed in our humanity.
You were immersed in the waters of the Jordan
as you are in our earthly life.

As the waters flowed all around you,
may we know that that you are forever about us.
As we are baptised in your Name,
may we know that we dwell in you and that you are in us.
Blessed are you, Lord Jesus Christ, with the Father and the Holy Spirit, One God now and for ever.
Amen.

Reading

Matthew 3:13–17

Hymn

Songs of thankfulness and praise *(Second verse)*

(Renew your baptismal vows and say the creed at this point, if appropriate.)

Special intention – in the light of God

We give thanks for the gift of water in Creation,
for rain, for rivers and seas, for pools and for oceans,
for the power of water to cleanse and refresh us,
for the life-giving properties of water,
for Jesus Christ immersed in the waters of the Jordan;
that our Lord is one with us and we dwell in him.
We rejoice in our own baptism
and that we are immersed in the Father, the Son and the Holy Spirit.

Closing prayer

God to enfold me,
God to surround me,
God in my speaking,
God in my thinking.

God in my sleeping,
God in my waking,
God in my watching,
God in my hoping.

God in my life,
God in my lips,
God in my soul,
God in my heart.

God in my sufficing,
God in my slumber,
God in mine ever-living soul,
God in mine eternity.
Carmina Gadelica III

Extinguish candle.

2 February

Candlemas

The presentation of Christ in the temple

If possible, everyone should be given a candle before starting.

Begin in the dark. If the room is not dark, close your eyes.

The darkness represents our world and our lives without Christ.

In the darkness ask all present to quietly invite Jesus the Light of the World into their lives.

Our bright shining candles are a sign of the divine splendour of the one who comes to expel the dark shadows of evil and to make the whole universe radiant with the brilliance of his eternal light. Our candles also show how bright our souls should be when we go to meet Christ.

The God-bearer, the most pure Virgin, carried the true Light in her arms and brought him to help those who lay in darkness. We too should carry a light for all to see and reflect the radiance of the true light as we hasten to meet him.

Indeed, this is the mystery we celebrate today: the light has come and has shone upon a world enveloped in shadows; the Dayspring from on high has visited us and given light to those who lived in darkness. This, then, is our feast, and we join in procession with lighted candles to reveal the light that has shone upon us and the glory that is yet to come to us through him. So let us hasten all together to meet our God.

The true light has come, the light that enlightens everyone who is born into this world. Let all of us be enlightened and made radiant by this light. Let all of us share in its splendour, and be so filled with it that no one remains in the darkness. Let us be shining ourselves as we go together to meet and to receive with the aged Simeon the light whose brilliance is eternal.

Sophronius of Jerusalem 6th–7th century

Welcome the light

The Lord is my light and my salvation; whom shall I fear?
The Lord is my light and my salvation.

The Lord is the stronghold of my life; of whom shall I be afraid?
The Lord is my light and my salvation.

Glory be to the Father, and to the Son, and to the Holy Spirit.
The Lord is my light and my salvation.

Psalm 27:1, 2

Candle-lighting

May Christ the Daystar dawn in our hearts
and triumph over the shades of night.

Jesus Christ is the Light of the World.
A light that no darkness can extinguish.

Light the candle.

Blessed are you, Lord God; to you be all praise and glory for ever and ever, for you are our light and our salvation. You created light out of darkness and have revealed your light and love in our lives through the birth of your Son, our Lord Jesus Christ. Blessed are you, Father, Son and Holy Spirit, one God for ever and ever.

If possible everyone present lights a candle or a taper from the lit candle and declares: **The Lord is my light and my salvation.**

Reading

Luke 2:22–40

Hymn

Christ, whose glory fills the skies

Special intention – in the light of God

Come, Lord of light:
Lighten our darkness;
Lighten our lives with your love;
Lighten our homes with your presence;
Lighten this world with your peace.
Come, Lord of Light, be known to be among us.

Closing prayer

Lord, as we move from here we are still in your presence,
your light is with us and before us.
Your light leads us and guides us.
In your light we live and move and have our being.
Your light will help us to banish the deeds of darkness.
As we extinguish this light, we rejoice that we dwell in your Light
and we are in your presence always.

Stay for a while rejoicing in the light of Christ.

Extinguish the candle.

Easter Day

Begin in the dark. If the room is not dark, close your eyes.

Welcome the light

Today we give thanks, for in dying Christ has conquered death; in rising to life again he has opened to us the way to everlasting life.

He has been raised from the dead, and indeed he is going ahead of you.
Matthew 28:7

As we meet in the love and light of the Father, the Son and the Holy Spirit, let us rejoice in the power of the resurrection.
Alleluia, Christ is risen.
He is risen indeed, Alleluia.

The Lord is here.
His Spirit is with us.

Candle-lighting

May Christ, risen in glory, scatter the darkness from our hearts and minds and from this world.
The light of the risen Christ shine upon us, this day and always.

Alleluia, Christ is risen.
He is risen indeed, Alleluia.

Light the candle.

Blessed are you, the God and Father of our Lord Jesus Christ; to you be glory and praise for ever. By raising your Son from the dead, death has been destroyed and new life has been restored. In him the victory over sin and the grave is won. May we live as 'Easter people', reflecting the glory of your resurrection. Blessed are you Father, Son and Holy Spirit.

Reading

Matthew 28:1–10

Hymn

Jesus lives! thy terrors now *(First two verses)*

Special intention – in the light of God

Risen Lord, we remember all who walk in darkness and who are burdened with troubles, the heavy-hearted and the sad. We ask your blessing upon all who are separated from their loved ones and who feel lonely or lost. We bring before you all who are ill and all who are fearful. We ask you to comfort all who stand by a graveside weeping, and all who mourn.
Risen Lord, make your presence known to us:
you are our light and our salvation. Alleluia.

Risen Lord, we ask that we might share in your resurrection and triumph over darkness and death. We ask your blessing upon our friends and loved ones who are departed from us. May they know of your power in the fullness of your kingdom. This day we rejoice that death is conquered: we are free, for you have won the victory.
Risen Lord, make your presence known to us:
you are our light and our salvation. Alleluia.

Closing prayer

Christ, you are risen from the dead.
We are risen with you.
May our life never deny this eternal life,
this peace and hope and joy.
Praise and glory to the God of life
who is stronger than all kinds of death. Alleluia.

A New Zealand Prayer Book

Extinguish candle.

We are Easter people;
alleluia is our song.

Easter 2
The Risen Lord and Mary

Begin in the dark. If the room is not dark, close your eyes.

Welcome the light

Today we give thanks, for in dying Christ has conquered death; in rising to life again he has opened to us the way to everlasting life.

She turned round and saw Jesus standing there, but she did not know it was Jesus.

John 20:14

As we meet in the love and light of the Father, the Son and the Holy Spirit, let us rejoice in the power of the resurrection.
Alleluia, Christ is risen.
He is risen indeed, Alleluia.

The Lord is here.
His Spirit is with us.

Candle-lighting

May Christ, risen in glory, scatter the darkness from our hearts and minds and from this world.
The light of the risen Christ shine upon us, this day and always.

Alleluia, Christ is risen.
He is risen indeed, Alleluia.

Light the candle.

Blessed are you, the God and Father of our Lord Jesus Christ; to you be glory and praise for ever. By your raising your Son from the dead, death has been destroyed and new life has been restored. In him the victory over sin and the grave is won. We rejoice that you, risen Lord, appeared to Mary in the garden, transforming her sorrow into joy, that you sent her to your disciples to proclaim you are risen. May our lives reflect the glory of your resurrection. Blessed are you Father, Son and Holy Spirit.

Reading

John 19:41–20:18

Hymn

All in an Easter garden

Special intention – in the light of God

Lord, make us aware of your risen presence. Roll away the heaviness, the doubt, the fear from our hearts. Fill our lives with the knowledge of your presence and your love, that our whole being may rejoice. Give us the courage to go out and to proclaim your love and your saving power. Lord, as we rejoice in your resurrection, we ask your blessing upon all who celebrate your presence, all who know you as the risen Lord. We pray for all who seek you and all who want to be close to you. Risen Lord, strengthen your Church to tell the Good News to the whole world.
Risen Lord, make your presence known to us:
you are our light and our salvation. Alleluia.

Risen Lord, as you appeared to Mary, may we know your presence in our homes and in all our dealings. Let us walk and work in your presence and seek to reveal your glory in the world. We ask you to bless all our loved ones and friends and keep us all ever in your love and in the power of your resurrection.
Risen Lord, make your presence known to us:
you are our light and our salvation.

Closing prayer

The whole bright world rejoices now:
with laughing cheer! with boundless joy!
The birds do sing on every bough:
Alleluia.

Then shout beneath the racing skies:
with laughing cheer! with boundless joy!
To him who rose that we might rise:
Alleluia.

Easter carol, 17th century

Extinguish candle.

We are Easter people;
alleluia is our song.

Easter 3
The risen Lord and the ten disciples

Begin in the dark. If the room is not dark, close your eyes.

Welcome the light

Today we give thanks, for in dying Christ has conquered death; in rising to life again he has opened to us the way to everlasting life.

The disciples rejoiced when they saw the Lord.
John 20:20

As we meet in the love and light of the Father, the Son and the Holy Spirit, let us rejoice in the power of the resurrection.
Alleluia, Christ is risen.
He is risen indeed, Alleluia.

The Lord is here.
His Spirit is with us.

Candle-lighting

May Christ, risen in glory, scatter the darkness from our hearts and minds and from this world.
The light of the risen Christ shine upon us, this day and always.

Alleluia, Christ is risen.
He is risen indeed, Alleluia.

Light the candle.

Blessed are you, Lord God, by whose power our Lord Jesus is raised from the dead. In your presence is life and life eternal. In your power, death is conquered and the gate to eternal life is open. We rejoice that you appeared to the disciples in the upper room and that in your presence is the fullness of joy. Blessed are you Father, Son and Holy Spirit.

Reading

John 20:19–23

Hymn

Jesus, stand among us in thy risen power

Special intention – in the light of God

Risen Lord, come stand among us that we may know you and love you, that we may love you and worship you, that we may worship you and serve you today and always.
Risen Lord, as you came to the disciples in an ordinary home, be known in our homes.
Come, risen Lord; be known among us and our loved ones:
come, enter our darkness and fears with your light:
come, break into all that would imprison us and set us free:
come, to our fear of venturing, and send us out in the power of your Spirit.
Lord of life eternal, hear us
and grant us your peace.

Risen Lord, we remember in your presence all who are housebound and all whose lives are restricted through their surroundings. We ask your blessing upon all who are suffering from depression or anxiety, all who are awaiting operations or a doctor's diagnosis. We pray for all who are not at peace with themselves, their neighbours or with you. May we all in our weakness know of your love and saving power.
Lord of life eternal, hear us
and grant us your peace.

Closing prayer

Risen Christ, Prince of Peace, come among us.
As you appeared to your disciples in the closed room,
come into our lives.
Come, breathe into us your life-giving Spirit.
Come, grant us your peace.
Come, empower us to witness to your resurrection.
Come and be known among us.
We ask this for you are alive
and live and reign with the Father
and the Holy Spirit, one God for ever and ever.
Amen.

Extinguish candle.

We are Easter people;
alleluia is our song.

Easter 4
The risen Lord and Thomas

Begin in the dark. If the room is not dark, close your eyes.

Welcome the light

Today we give thanks, for in dying Christ has conquered death; in rising to life again he has opened to us the way to everlasting life.

Then he said to Thomas, 'Put your finger here and see my hands. Reach out your hand and put it in my side. Do not doubt but believe.'

John 20:27

As we meet in the love and light of the Father, the Son and the Holy Spirit, let us rejoice in the power of the resurrection.
Alleluia, Christ is risen.
He is risen indeed, Alleluia.

The Lord is here.
His Spirit is with us.

Candle-lighting

May Christ, risen in glory, scatter the darkness from our hearts and minds and from this world.
The light of the risen Christ shine upon us, this day and always.

Alleluia, Christ is risen.
He is risen indeed, Alleluia.

Light the candle.

Blessed are you, the God and Father of our Lord Jesus Christ; to you be glory and praise for ever. By the risen Lord appearing to Thomas you encourage us to wait upon you even in our doubts. You still come to us and give yourself to us, even though we may doubt you. Even when we turn away, you do not leave us. Help us to be aware of you in our lives and to give ourselves to you in love and in doing your will. Blessed are you, Father, Son and Holy Spirit.

Reading

John 20:24–31

Hymn

Love's redeeming work is done *(First two verses)*

Special intention – in the light of God

Thanksgiving
Holy and ever-living God, we give you thanks and praise that Christ is risen. In dying he has conquered death and in rising again he has opened for us the way to life eternal. Today we rejoice that you, Lord Christ, appeared to Thomas though he doubted your resurrection. We give thanks that you never leave us even when we doubt you or forget you. We thank you for all your faithful people, who, though they have not seen you, believe in you and reveal in their lives your risen power. Glory to you, risen Christ, with the Father and the Holy Spirit, one God now and for ever.
Amen.

Intercessions
Risen Lord, we ask your blessing upon all your faithful people, all those who confess you as their Lord and their God. We remember all who meet in your name and talk of your power. We pray for study groups and theological colleges, for all who meditate on your word and who seek your presence. We bring before you all who are beset by doubt and disbelief and all who are reaching out to seek you, to touch you and to find you. We pray especially for the Church in India. [1]
My Lord, and my God,
hear us and help us.

1. Tradition has it that St Thomas evangelized India.

Risen Lord, we remember before you all who have lost confidence in themselves or in others, those who have lost vision or trust. We ask your blessing upon all who are ill, all who have been injured in accidents or by acts of violence and upon all who have the care of them. Give them courage and hope amid their troubles.
Lord of life hear us
and grant us your peace.

Closing prayer

Jesus, King of glory, you are our Lord and our God:
as you appeared to Thomas, come to us.
Come to our darkness with your light,
come to our doubting with your presence.
In your death you have triumphed over death:
come to us with the gift of life-eternal.
Grant that by your wounded hands and side
we may know your love and your healing power.
Come, Lord, in the power of your Spirit,
fill us with your peace.
We ask this for your love's sake,
O Christ, who with the Father
and the Holy Spirit lives and reigns for ever.
Amen.

Extinguish candle.

We are Easter people;
alleluia is our song.

Easter 5
The risen Lord on the road to Emmaus

Begin in the dark. If the room is not dark, close your eyes.

Welcome the light

Today we give thanks, for in dying Christ has conquered death; in rising to life again he has opened to us the way to everlasting life.

Were not our hearts burning within us while he was talking to us on the road, while he was opening the scriptures to us?

Luke 24:32

As we meet in the love and light of the Father, the Son and the Holy Spirit, let us rejoice in the power of the resurrection.
Alleluia, Christ is risen.
He is risen indeed, Alleluia.

The Lord is here.
His Spirit is with us.

Candle-lighting

May Christ, risen in glory, scatter the darkness from our hearts and minds and from this world.
The light of the risen Christ shine upon us, this day and always.

Alleluia, Christ is risen.
He is risen indeed, Alleluia.

Light the candle.

Blessed are you, Lord Christ, for you are with us in our journeying and in our resting. You are to be found in our homes and our daily

lives. You make yourself known to us in the breaking of the bread. You, Lord, are our hope and our strength; in you we trust. Blessed are you, Christ our Saviour, with the Father and Holy Spirit, one God for ever and ever.
Amen.

Reading

Luke 24:13–35

Hymn

Abide with me *(First verse)*

Special intention – in the light of God

We rejoice that you, Lord Christ, appeared to Cleopas and his companion; you walked with them, talked with them, revealed the Scriptures to them and were known to them in the breaking of the bread. In your presence their hearts were filled with joy. We thank you that you can still be known through the Scriptures and the breaking of the bread. Glory to you, risen Christ, with the Father and the Holy Spirit, one God now and for ever.
Amen.

Risen Lord, make yourself known to us and abide with us.
Travel with us as we journey through life.
Be known to us when our hearts are weary, and enlighten us.
Reveal your presence to us through the Scriptures
and through the sharing of meals together.
Bless all who seek to tell of your presence
through words or through their example.

We pray for preachers and teachers of the faith and for all Christians who witness through their lives. We remember before you all who feel they are in the dark and have lost any sense or awareness of your love and presence.
Christ, with us now,
hear us and help us.

Risen Lord, make yourself known
and abide with all who are making momentous journeys,
all who are on the move because they have no place to call their own.
Abide with and bless all refugees and displaced peoples,
all who are caught up in war or in acts of violence or tyranny.
Abide with those who have lost their homes and their work,
all who are unemployed and who are finding life hard.
Jesus, with us now,
abide with us and help us.

Risen Lord, make yourself known and abide with us.
Abide with us when our hearts burn within us,
may we know that you are near,
and set our hearts on fire with love for you.
Abide with all who are world-weary,
the disillusioned, and the confused;
may they know that you abide with them in their troubles
and that you are their hope and salvation.
Jesus, with us now,
abide with us and help us.

Closing prayer

Abide with us, O Lord, today and to eternity.
Abide with us in our joys and in our sorrows.
Abide with us in our success and in our failures.
Abide with us in darkness and in the light.
Abide with us in love and your salvation.
Abide with us now and to eternity.

Extinguish candle.

We are Easter people;
alleluia is our song.

Easter 6
The risen Lord on the shore

Begin in the dark. If the room is not dark, close your eyes.

Welcome the light

Today we give thanks, for in dying Christ has conquered death; in rising to life again he has opened to us the way to everlasting life.

Just after daybreak, Jesus stood on the beach; but the disciples did not know that it was Jesus.

John 21:4

As we meet in the love and light of the Father, the Son and the Holy Spirit, let us rejoice in the power of the resurrection.
Alleluia, Christ is risen.
He is risen indeed, Alleluia.

The Lord is here.
His Spirit is with us.

Candle-lighting

May Christ, risen in glory, scatter the darkness from our hearts and minds and from this world.
The light of the risen Christ shine upon us, this day and always.

Alleluia, Christ is risen.
He is risen indeed, Alleluia.

Light the candle.

Blessed are you God and Father of our Lord Jesus Christ, to you be praise and glory for ever. Alleluia. By the raising of your Son from the dead you have opened to us the way to eternal life. As our Lord came to the disciples while they were fishing, he comes to us this day and every day, in our work, and in our sharing together. He is to be met and to be acknowledged as our Lord. In him, you have given us an everlasting joy. Blessed are you Father, Son and Holy Spirit.

Reading

John 21:1–25

Hymn

Newness *(to the tune 'Angel Voices')*
Fishermen who toiled for nothing
on the lake all night
hear the sound of Jesus' welcome
in the morning light:
in the friendship shared at breakfast
old mistakes are lost to sight.

Every day a fresh beginning -
newness, come what may!
In the most unlikely places
Jesus reigns today;
from the past to new horizons
Christ our Saviour leads the way.
Martin E. Leckebusch

Special intention – in the light of God

Lord Jesus, we rejoice that you appeared to the disciples in their work and on the seashore. We give thanks that we can meet you in our daily routine, in our work and in our travels. We praise you for all who have met you on the shores of time and of eternity. Glory to you, risen Christ, with the Father and the Holy Spirit, one God now and for ever.
Amen.

Risen Lord, we rejoice that you come to us.
You fill our emptiness with the glory of your presence.
You call us out of darkness into the light of eternal life.
As you show us your love, you ask us to follow you.
May we heed your call and follow you.
Risen Christ, ever near,
hear us and help us.

Risen Lord, be seen
among all who work hard for little gain,
among all whose work is dreary,
among all whose lives seem fruitless or meaningless.
Bless all who toil to provide us with our daily food,
especially fishermen and all who work upon the sea.
Risen Christ, ever near,
hear us and help us.

Closing prayer

Lord of life, come, touch our lives;
walk the borders of our world.
Come to us in our emptiness;
come with your joyfulness.
Come to us in our struggles;
come with your peace.
Come to us in our sinfulness;
come with your forgiveness.
Come Lord in time
and bring us to eternal life.

Extinguish candle.

We are Easter people;
alleluia is our song.

Candle
Prayers

Ascension

Begin in the dark. If the room is not dark, close your eyes.

Welcome the light

We give thanks, for in dying Christ has conquered death; in his ascension he has opened to us the way to everlasting life.

While he was blessing them, he withdrew from them and was carried up into heaven.

Luke 24:51

As we meet in the love and light of the Father, the Son and the Holy Spirit, let us rejoice in the power of his resurrection and ascension.
Alleluia, Christ is risen.
He is risen indeed, Alleluia.

The Lord is here.
His Spirit is with us.

Candle-lighting

May Christ, risen in glory, scatter the darkness from our hearts and minds and from this world.
The presence of the ascended Christ be with us, this day and always.

Alleluia, Christ is risen.
He is risen indeed, Alleluia.

Light the candle.

Blessed are you, Lord our God,
for you have raised your Son from the darkness of death
to the fullness of life eternal, to your right hand on high.

By his death he has destroyed death;
by his rising to life again he has restored to us eternal life;
by his ascension he has opened for us the gate of glory.
Blessed are you Father, Son and Holy Spirit.

Reading

Luke 24:44–53

Hymn

Hail the day that sees him rise *(First two verses)*

Special intention – in the light of God

As we rejoice in your ascension, O Christ,
we give you thanks for men and women of vision,
for those who have shared the light of their faith with us.
We remember all whose lives are clouded by doubt or despair,
all who walk in darkness.
Lord, be known to those who feel life is dull and empty,
that they may come to know your joy, ascended Lord.

Closing prayer

Ascended Lord, to you be praise and glory.
We come to you in love
and give our hearts to you.
As you are in heaven,
heaven and our hearts are one.
Ascended Lord, to you be praise and glory.

Extinguish candle.

We are Easter people;
alleluia is our song.

Sunday after the Ascension

Begin in the dark. If the room is not dark, close your eyes.

Welcome the light

We give thanks, for in dying Christ has conquered death; in his ascension he has opened to us the way to everlasting life.

As they were watching, he was lifted up, and a cloud took him out of their sight.

Acts 1:9

As we meet in the love and light of the Father, the Son and the Holy Spirit, let us rejoice in the power of his resurrection and ascension.
Alleluia, Christ is risen.
He is risen indeed, Alleluia.

The Lord is here.
His Spirit is with us.

Candle-lighting

May Christ, risen in glory, scatter the darkness from our hearts and minds and from this world.
The presence of the ascended Christ be with us, this day and always.

Alleluia, Christ is risen.
He is risen indeed, Alleluia.

Light the candle.

God of all, we give you thanks and praise for the glorious ascension of Christ our Lord. In his death he has triumphed over death.

In his rising to life again he has opened to us the way to eternal life. In his glorious ascension he who came down has returned to the fullness of his kingdom. He came down for us and now we are raised with him. We praise you, for we are ever in your presence and you give your Spirit to us. Lord, may we learn to rejoice in the reality that we dwell in you and know that you dwell in us. To you be glory and praise for ever, Father, Son and Holy Spirit.

Reading

Acts 1:6–11

Hymn

The head that once was crowned with thorns *(First three verses)*

Special intention – in the light of God

Risen and ascended Christ,
may our hearts be with you, for then our hearts are in heaven.
We wait upon the gift of the Spirit
that we may be guided and empowered to do what you would have us do:
that we may be the people you want us to be
and that we may share in your mission of love to the world.
We ask your blessing upon all who are being baptised or confirmed at this time,
all who are seeking to be ordained; may we all be Spirit-filled and charismatic people.
Risen and ascended Christ,
King of glory, give us of your Holy Spirit.

Risen and ascended Christ,
may your Holy Spirit come and refresh and renew us:
that those who are down may be lifted up:
that the downtrodden may arise to a new freedom:
that all ill, those suffering from handicaps or disabilities may find new hope.

We ask your blessing upon all who use their gifts to relieve suffering and to bring healing.
Risen and ascended Christ,
King of glory, give us of your Holy Spirit.

Closing prayer

Christ, you came down
that we might rise with you.
Christ, you share our humanity
that we may partake of your Divinity.
Christ, you ascended into heaven
that we might be one with you in your kingdom.
Christ, risen and ascended,
may we abide with you for ever.

Extinguish candle.

We are Easter people;
alleluia is our song.

Pentecost

Begin in the dark. If the room is not dark, close your eyes.

Welcome the light

We rejoice this day in the coming of the Holy Spirit.

Divided tongues, as of fire, appeared among them, and a tongue rested on each of them. All of them were filled with the Holy Spirit.

Acts 2:3, 4

Candle-lighting

I light this candle for us, for God gives us the gift of his Spirit who came upon the disciples in tongues of flame.
Alleluia, the Lord is here
his Spirit is with us, Alleluia.

We are Easter people;
alleluia is our song.

Light the candle.

Blessed are you, Lord our God; to you be praise and glory for ever.
At the beginning of creation
your Spirit brought order out of chaos
and a world out of your love.
In the power of the Spirit you breathed life into the world
and all creation rejoiced in your love.
We thank you for the gift of life
and that your Spirit is with us and within us.
As we give you praise, pour your Spirit upon us
and set our hearts on fire with love for you,
Father, Son and Holy Spirit.
Amen.

Reading

Acts 2:1–21

Hymn

Come down, O Love divine *(First two verses)*

Special intention – in the light of God

Come, Holy Spirit, breath of God and renew us and inspire us.
Come, Holy Spirit, wind of God, refresh us and move us to do what is right.
Come, Holy Spirit, fire of God, warm our hearts and disperse all dullness and coldness.
Come, Holy Spirit, power of God, enable us and help us to live to your glory.
Come, Holy Spirit, as you did to the disciples.
Holy Spirit, come upon us:
and inspire us.

Come, Holy Spirit, inspire peoples and nations with your gift of peace.
Come, Holy Spirit, guide and give vision to all artists, musicians and craftspeople.
Come, Holy Spirit, enlighten and direct all research workers, scientists, and conservationists.
Come, Holy Spirit, upon all who seek to care for the world, its beauty and its environment.
Holy Spirit, come upon us:
and inspire us.

Come Holy Spirit,
as you filled the house where the disciples were,
fill our homes and our hearts.
Let us know that we dwell in you and that you are in us.
Holy Spirit, come upon us:
and inspire us.

Closing prayer

Breathe in us, Holy Spirit,
that we may think what is holy.
Move in us, Holy Spirit,
that we may do what is holy.
Attract us, Holy Spirit,
that we may love what is holy.
Strengthen us, Holy Spirit,
that we may guard what is holy.
Guard us, Holy Spirit,
that we may keep what is holy.

St Augustine of Hippo 354 – 430

Extinguish candle.

Trinity

Begin in the dark. If the room is not dark, close your eyes.

Welcome the light

We rejoice today in the threefold nature of our God.

The grace of our Lord Jesus Christ, the love of God, and the communion of the Holy Spirit be with all of you.

2 Corinthians 13:13

Do you believe in God the Creator who made heaven and earth, who made us out of love?
I believe and trust in him.

Do you believe in God the Son, who shared in our humanity, who died and rose again for us?
I believe and trust in him.

Do you believe in God the Holy Spirit, who is the Lord and giver of life and sustains us in our need?
I believe and trust in him.

This is the faith of the whole Church.
I believe and love one God, Father, Son and Holy Spirit.

Candle-lighting

We light this candle as an expression of the love of God for us and that he gives light to our lives.

Jesus Christ is the Light of the World.
A light that no darkness can quench.

Light the candle.

Blessed be God, Father, Son and Holy Spirit,
the Three in One, the holy and wonderful Trinity
bound together in one eternity of love.
Blessed be God, the creator of all things.
Blessed be the Christ, our Saviour and Friend.
Blessed be the Spirit within us, our Guide and Strength.
Blessed be God, for all that he is and all he has done.
Blessed be the One and the Three.
Blessed be God for ever.

Reading

John 16:12–15

Hymn

Father of heaven, whose love profound

Special intention – in the light of God

Father, we give you thanks for your creation, for the beauty and wonder of our world. We ask your blessing upon all who work in caring for the earth and who labour to provide us with our daily needs.
Holy, holy, holy God,
hear us and help us.

Jesus Christ, Son of God, we give thanks for your love revealed in our salvation. May we share with you in the bringing of all people to a greater freedom. We ask your blessing upon all who are caring for the ill and the hungry of our world.
Holy, holy, holy God,
hear us and help us.

Holy Spirit of God, may we know your presence with us and within us. We give thanks for the talents and the abilities you give to us. We pray for all scientists and research workers; for all artists and craftspeople.
Holy, holy, holy God,
hear us and help us.

Closing prayer

I live today in the power of the Father.
I live today in the love of the Saviour.
I live today in the light of the Spirit.
I live today in newness of life.
I live today in freshness and renewal.
I live today in time and for eternity.
I live today in the grace and goodness of the Holy Trinity.

Extinguish candle.

Candle Prayers

Transfiguration

Begin in the dark. If the room is not dark, close your eyes.

Welcome the light

In their spending time alone with Jesus on the mountain, Peter, James and John became aware of his glory.

The Word became flesh and lived among us, and we have seen his glory, the glory as of a father's only son, full of grace and truth.

John 1:14

Candle-lighting

We light this candle as an expression of the glory of God, revealed in the face of Jesus Christ; asking that our lives may burn with his glory.

Jesus Christ is the Light of the World.
A light that no darkness can quench.

Light the candle.

Blessed are you, Lord our God,
for you have revealed yourself through Moses and the prophets.
You have made yourself known to us through your saints,
but above all you show us your glory in the face of our Lord
Jesus Christ.
As we open our lives to his glory may we reflect it in all the world.
Blessed are you, Father, Son and Holy Spirit.

Reading

Luke 9:28–36

Hymn

Christ, whose glory fills the skies

Special intention – in the light of God

Lord, change us and we shall be changed.
Transform our homes into places of your glory.
Transform our lives to reveal your presence.
Transform our minds to know your peace.
Transform our hearts to abide in your love.
May we know you are always with our loved ones and with us.
God, in your goodness,
grant us a glimpse of your glory.

Lord, change us and we shall be changed.
Transform our darkness with your light.
Transform our weakness with your strength.
Transform our fear by your protection.
Transform our loneliness by your presence.
Transform us that we may reflect your glory.
God, in your goodness,
grant us a glimpse of your glory.

Closing prayer

Awaken us to your glory:
dispel the darkness of night;
destroy the heaviness of heart;
cure the blindness of sight;
heal the deafness of ears;
open the mouth that is dumb;
restore a gentleness of touch;
encourage a sense of adventure;
bring us an awareness of you.
Awaken us to your glory.

Extinguish candle.

All Saints

Begin in the dark. If the room is not dark, close your eyes.

Welcome the light

Today we rejoice in the Communion of Saints and give thanks to God for all who have witnessed to his love and power.

The holy ones of the Most High shall receive the kingdom and possess the kingdom for ever – for ever and ever.

Daniel 7:18

Candle-lighting

As we light the candle, we rejoice in the fellowship of the saints in light.

Jesus Christ is the Light of the World.
A light that no darkness can quench.

Light the candle.

Blessed are you, Lord our God,
for you have called us to share in the fellowship of all your saints.
Grant that in the darkness that is about us
we may be guided by their example
and so serve you in love and in peace.
Blessed are you, Father, Son and Holy Spirit.

Reading

1 Corinthians 1:26–31

Hymn

For all the saints *(First three verses)*

Special intention – in the light of God

Rejoicing in the fellowship of all the saints, we pray to the Lord:
Lord, make us to be numbered with your saints,
in your eternal glory.

Blessed God, we remember before you
all who have set us an example by their grace and goodness.
We ask your blessing upon our homes and families.
We pray for all who are suffering from broken relationships and all who feel lonely.
Lord, make us to be numbered with your saints,
in your eternal glory.

Blessed God, we remember before you
all who have suffered persecution for their faith.
We ask you to bless those who strive against injustice and evil.
We pray for all who suffer from tyranny or oppression.
Lord, make us to be numbered with your saints,
in your eternal glory.

Closing prayer

Dearest Lord, teach me to be generous;
teach me to serve you as you deserve;
to give and not to count the cost,
to fight and not to heed the wounds,
to toil and not to seek for rest,
to labour and not to seek a reward,
save that of knowing that I do your will.

Ignatius Loyola 1491–1556

Extinguish candle.

Birth

Begin in the dark. If the room is not dark, close your eyes.

Welcome the light

Behold, children are a heritage from the Lord, the fruit of the womb is a reward.

Psalm 127:3 (NKJV)

Holy God, we give you thanks for the gift of life and especially the life of this child who is given to us. As you created us all out of love, may we pour our love on this child who is yours and ours.

Candle-lighting

As we light this candle, we give thanks to God for life in his light.
Jesus Christ is the Light of the World.
A light that no darkness can quench.

Light the candle.

Blessed are you, Lord our God,
for you give life and love to all of your creatures.
We rejoice in the gift of our lives
and in the life of this newborn child.
We lift *her* up to you and ask your blessing upon *her*.
Blessed are you, Father, Son and Holy Spirit.

Reading

Luke 2:8–20

Hymn

For the beauty of the earth *(First three verses)*

Special intention – in the light of God

Praise, glory and thanksgiving are yours, O Lord.
You are the giver of life and life eternal.
You have created us, and give your Spirit to us.
Be known to be with *(name)*
in *her* joys and in *her* sorrows,
in sickness and in health,
in *her* successes and in *her* failures,
in *her* home and in *her* travels.
Bless *her* with your love now and for evermore.

Closing prayer

God, we give you thanks and praise for life.
We rejoice in the gift of this child to us.
Holy Father, be *her* strength.
Lord Jesus, be *her* protector.
Holy Spirit, be *her* guide.
Father, Son and Holy Spirit, be always with *her*,
and keep *her* in your peace.

Extinguish candle.

Journeying

Begin in the dark. If the room is not dark, close your eyes.

Welcome the light

We rejoice in the presence of God and light a candle to remind us that God goes with us wherever we travel.

God said: 'My presence will go with you, and I will give you rest.'
Exodus 33:14

Candle-lighting

Jesus Christ is the Light of the World.
A light that no darkness can quench.

Light the candle.

Blessed are you, Lord our God, for you have created all things and formed us in your own image. Wherever we travel we can see your works and know that you are with us. In everyone we meet we have the opportunity of seeing your image and encountering your presence. In all our journeying you are there, ever present, ready to guide, support and direct us. Blessed are you, Father, Son and Holy Spirit.

Readings

Psalm 139:1–18

Hymn

One more step along the world I go

The path of right
My walk this day with God,
my walk this day with Christ,
my walk this day with Spirit,
the Threefold all kindly:
Ho! ho! ho! the Threefold all kindly.

My shielding this day from ill,
my shielding this night from harm,
ho! ho! both my soul and my body,
be by Father, by Son, by Holy Spirit.

Be the Father shielding me,
be the Son shielding me,
be the Spirit shielding me,
as Three and as One:
Ho! ho! ho! as Three and as One.

Carmina Gadelica III:49

Special intention – in the light of God

God, you seek us when we hide:
to you we sing our songs of praise.

God, you meet us when we seek:
to you we sing our songs of praise.

God, you called Abram to walk into the unknown:
to you we sing our songs of praise.

God, you led Moses through the desert:
to you we sing our songs of praise.

God, you encouraged Joshua to 'go forward':
to you we sing our songs of praise.

God, you travel with all your people:
to you we sing our songs of praise.

We ask your blessing upon people who are on the move.
We remember those who are leaving home or setting up a new home.
We bring before you the homeless, the refugees and all displaced persons.
We remember all who are setting off for new places of work, or to do new projects.

We remember all who are travelling in places of danger,
all who are weary, all who have lost their way, all who are in the dark.
God, companion of all, make yourself known to each in their journey
that their 'hearts may burn within them' with your love.

Closing prayer

May the strength of God pilot us.
May the power of God preserve us.
May the wisdom of God instruct us.
May the hand of God protect us.
May the way of God direct us.
May the shield of God defend us.
May the host of God guard us.

Attributed to St Patrick

Extinguish candle.

Candle
Prayers

Loved ones leaving

Begin in the dark. If the room is not dark, close your eyes.

Welcome the light

We rejoice in our love for each other and know that wherever we go we are in the love of God.

Jesus said: 'Remember I am with you always, to the end of the age.'

Matthew 28:20

Candle-lighting

Jesus Christ is the Light of the World.
A light that no darkness can quench.

Light the candle.

Blessed are you, Lord our God,
for you created us out of love and for your love.
You have commanded that we love one another
as you have loved us.
Grant that, as we grow in love,
we may grow in our awareness of you
and of your great love for us.
Blessed are you, Father, Son and Holy Spirit.

Reading

1 John 4:7–12

Hymn

God be with you till we meet again

Special intention – in the light of God

God of love, we remember before you
all who are separated from loved ones
through illness, war, or occupation.
God of love,
be with us.

God of love, we bring before you
all who are struggling with their relationships,
all who are lonely and all who feel deserted.
God of love,
be with us.

God of love, we give you thanks for our home,
for each of our loved ones,
and all who are dear to us.
God of love,
be with us.

God of love, ask your blessing on *(name),*
as *she* leaves for *(place or reason).*
May *she* know *she* is enfolded in your love
and is ever under your protection.
God of love,
be with us.

Closing prayer

The love of God go with you.
The peace of God be upon you.
God go behind you to protect you.
God go before you to guide you.
God be there to welcome you.
God be on your left to defend you.
God be on your right to strengthen you.
God be beneath you to uphold you.
God be above you to raise you up.
God be within you and about you,
until we meet again.

Extinguish candle.

In times of darkness

Begin in the dark. If the room is not dark, close your eyes.

Welcome the light

The people who walked in darkness have seen a great light; they who lived in a land of deep darkness, on them the light has shined.

Isaiah 9:2

Come, Lord of Life,
come with your light.
Come, enter the darkness of my life.
Come, that I may walk in the light of your Love.
Come, that I may walk in the newness of this day.

Candle-lighting

In our darkness we are not alone; the Lord of Light is ever present.

Jesus Christ is the Light of the World.
A light that no darkness can extinguish.

Light the candle.

Reading

Isaiah 4:1–3 or Psalm 23

Hymn

Lead us, heavenly Father, lead us

Special intention – in the light of God

Holy God, holy and Strong One, in my emptiness I come to be filled by you.
Lord, you are my light and my salvation.

Holy God, holy and Strong One, in my darkness I come to your light.
Lord, you are my light and my salvation.

Holy God, holy and Strong One, in my troubles I come to your love.
Lord, you are my light and my salvation.

Holy God, holy and Strong One, in my illness I come for your healing.
Lord, you are my light and my salvation.

Holy God, holy and Strong One, in my need I come to your salvation.
Lord, you are my light and my salvation.

Lord, you know my needs before I ask
and are always more ready to give than I desire or deserve.
I come to rest in the love of your presence.
I come for renewal and refreshment.
I come for the fullness of life-eternal.
Amen.

Closing prayer

Lord, you love me
with an everlasting love.
When I lose sight of you,
your eye is upon me.
When I lose hold on you,
you enfold me in your love.
When I am in the dark,
the light of your presence is with me.
Lord, you love me
with an everlasting love.
Light incomprehensible, of dazzling brightness,
surround me with the radiance of your glory.

Extinguish candle.

A light for someone

Begin in the dark. If the room is not dark, close your eyes.

Welcome the light

Today we light a candle for *(name)* that *he* may know the light and love of God.

Walk while you have the light, so that the darkness will not overtake you. If you walk in the darkness, you do not know where you are going. While you have the light, believe in the light, so that you may become children of light.

John 12:35, 36

Candle-lighting

Jesus Christ is the Light of the World.
A light that no darkness can quench.

Light the candle.

Blessed are you, Lord our God, for you love us with an everlasting love. You care for all of your creation and you are with us always. May your love and your presence be known to *(name)* that *he* may walk in your light and live in your peace. Blessed are you, Father, Son and Holy Spirit.

(Name),
may the blessing of light be upon you,
light about you,
light within you.
May the Christ light shine upon you,
warm your heart
and shine from your eyes.

Reading

Psalm 121

Hymn

Thou, whose almighty word

Special intention – in the light of God

God of light, we ask you to guide,
to enlighten,
to fill with your radiance
our loved one this day.

God of love, we ask you to embrace,
to be with,
to fill with your love
our loved one this day.

God of peace, we ask you to calm,
to give rest to,
to support,
our loved one this day.

Closing prayer

Lord, fill *(name)*:
fill *him* with your peace.
Fill *him* with your presence.

Lord, fill *(name)*:
fill *him* with your grace.
Fill *him* with your goodness.

Lord, fill *(name)*:
fill *him* with your love.
Fill *him* with your light.

Extinguish candle, or, if this is a votive candle in a safe place, you may choose to say far fewer words and let the candle burn as your prayer. God knows our needs. Leave the candle burning, knowing he hears you.

For the departed

This service can be used on All Souls' Day, 2 November.

Begin in the dark. If the room is not dark, close your eyes.

Welcome the light

We rejoice this day that in Christ Jesus light has conquered darkness and life has triumphed over death.

Jesus said: 'I am the resurrection and the life. Those who believe in me, though they die, will live, and everyone who lives and believes in me will never die.'

John 11:25, 26

Candle-lighting

Jesus Christ is the Light of the World.
A light no darkness can quench.

Light the candle.

Blessed be the Lord, the God of Israel,
for he has looked favourably on his people and redeemed them.
He has raised up a mighty saviour for us
In the house of his servant David.

By the tender compassion of our God,
the dawn from on high will break upon us,
to shine on those who sit in darkness and the shadow of death:
to guide our feet into the way of peace.

From the Song of Zechariah, Luke 1:68, 69, 78, 79

Reading

1 Corinthians 15:35–58

Give rest, O Christ, to thy servant with thy saints:
where sorrow and pain are no more;
neither sighing but life everlasting.
Thou only art immortal, the creator and maker of man:
and we are mortal formed from the dust of the earth,
and unto earth shall we return:
for so thou didst ordain,
when thou created me saying:
'Dust thou art and unto dust shalt thou return.'
All we go down to the dust;
and weeping o'er the grave we make our song:
Alleluia, alleluia, alleluia.
Give rest, O Christ, to thy servant with thy saints:
where sorrow and pain are no more;
neither sighing but life everlasting.

Russian Kontakion for the Dead

Special intention – in the light of God

O God, Creator and Giver of life and life eternal,
have mercy upon us.

O Christ, triumphing over death, and our Redeemer,
have mercy upon us.

O Holy Spirit, Breath of Life, and Restorer,
have mercy upon us.

O Holy and Blessed Trinity
have mercy upon us.

Give rest, O Lord, to your servant with your saints:
Lord, hear us.

Grant that *she* may be where sorrow and sighing are no more:
Lord, hear us.

That *she* may come to see you and know you:
Lord, hear us.

That *she* may love you and serve you:
Lord, hear us.

That *she* may enjoy the presence in the fullness of your kingdom:
Lord, hear us.

That *she* may abide with you for ever:
Lord, hear us.

That we may see that our end is no end:
Lord, hear us.

That we may know that, in you, life is eternal
Lord, hear us.

Blessed are you, Lord our God,
for with you are the resurrection and the life:
with you are the rest and peace of our loved ones departed:
in you is our hope and trust:
blessed are you, Father, Son and Holy Spirit
for ever and ever.
Amen.

Closing prayer

We give them back to you, dear Lord, who gave them to us. You did not lose them in giving, so we have not lost them by their return. What you gave you take not away, O Lover of Souls; for what is yours is ours also if we are yours. Your Son has taught us that life is eternal and love is immortal, and death is only an horizon, and an horizon is nothing save the limit of our sight. Lift us up, strong Son of God, that we may see further; cleanse our eyes that we may see more clearly; and draw us closer to yourself that we may know ourselves to be nearer to our loved ones who are with thee. And while thou dost prepare for us, prepare us also for that happy place that, where they are and you are, we too may be for evermore, O dear Lord of life and death.

William Penn 1644–1718

May we live as those who believe in
the love and the presence of God;
the forgiveness of sins;
that, in Christ, life is eternal;
and the blessing of God Almighty, the Father, the Son and the Holy Spirit be upon us and upon our loved ones departed, now and for evermore.
Amen.

Extinguish candle.

Copyright Acknowledgements

The publishers wish to thank all those who have given their pemission to reproduce copyright material in this publication.

Every effort has been made to trace the owners of copyright material and we hope that no copyright has been infringed. Pardon is sought and apology made if the contrary be the case, and a correction will be made in any reprint of this book.

Also by David Adam

The Great I Am
Product Code: 1501135

A Prayer a Day from Advent to Epiphany
Product Code: 1501112

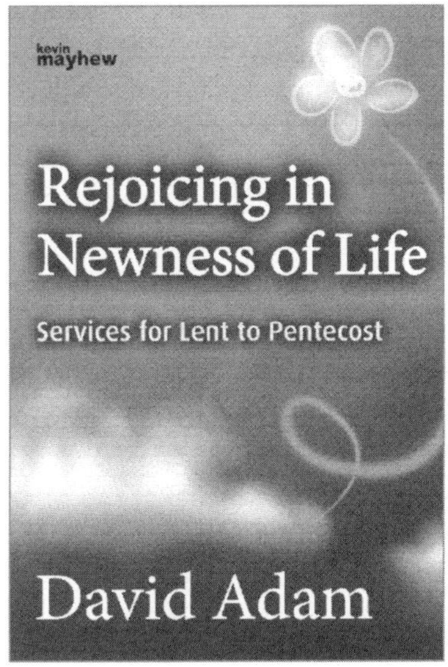

Rejoicing in Newness of Life

Product Code: 1501205

1000 Prayers for Public worship

Product Code: 1501128

Welcoming The Light
Product Code: 1501195

Daily Prayer
Product Code: 1501124